MW01121571

Your Top Students

Classroom strategies that meet the needs of the gifted

SHIRLEY TAYLOR

Foreword by
CHERYLL DUQUETTE

Pembroke Publishers Limited

Pembroke Publishers
538 Hood Road
Markham, Ontario, Canada L3R 3K9
www.pembrokepublishers.com

Distributed in the U.S. by Stenhouse Publishers
477 Congress Street
Portland, ME 04101
www.stenhouse.com

© 2003 User Friendly Resources

All rights reserved.
No part of this publication may be reproduced in any form or by any means
electronic or mechanical, including photocopy, recording, or any information,
storage or retrieval system, without permission in writing from the publisher.

Every effort has been made to contact copyright holders for permission to
reproduce borrowed material. The publishers apologize for any such omissions
and will be pleased to rectify them in subsequent reprints of the book.

This edition is adapted from a book originally published in Australia by User
Friendly Resources — www.userfr.com.

We acknowledge the financial support of the Government of Canada through
the Book Publishing Industry Development Program (BPIDP) for our
publishing activities.

We acknowledge the Government of Ontario through the Ontario Media
Development Corporation's Ontario Book Initiative.

Canadian Cataloguing in Publication Data

Taylor, Shirley
   Your top students / Shirley Taylor; edited by Cheryll Duquette. —
Canadian ed.

Previously published under title: Gifted and talented children.
Includes bibliographical references and index.
ISBN 1-55138-159-1

   1. Gifted children — Education. I. Duquette, Cheryll. II. Title.

LC3993.22.T39 2003   371.95   C2003-903411-9

Editor: Kathryn Cole, Pauline Scanlan
Cover Design: John Zehethofer
Cover Photography: Photo Disk
Typesetting: Jay Tee Graphics Ltd.

Printed and bound in Canada
9 8 7 6 5 4 3 2 1

Contents

Foreword

In most elementary schools, children with exceptionalities are taught in regular classrooms alongside their peers. In the course of a day, a teacher may struggle to provide accommodations for students with behavior problems, learning disabilities, physical challenges, and language barriers. Unfortunately, teachers may not identify, or know what to do with students who are academically gifted. Often, gifted students end up being "classroom helpers" or "silent readers" while they wait for the rest of the class to "catch up". Although up to 5 per cent of the population may be considered gifted, this is one group of students that is under served in schools, despite the fact that many have Individual Education Plans (IEPs), and have a legal right to an appropriate education.

Many teachers argue that their time and effort should be focused on those who need remedial work and not those who seem to have an abundance of ability. This seems to imply that gifted students do not need accommodations because they are smart enough to take care of themselves. Nothing could be farther from the truth. How many times have you encountered a student who has completed seatwork perfectly within five minutes? If that student becomes bored, he or she may begin to bother classmates, fidget, or act out. Over time, the teacher may begin to treat the student as a "behavior problem" which can cause low self-esteem and escalate the problem. Moreover, when students are not challenged, they develop the belief that they don't need to work to get good marks. When they enter university the workload becomes overwhelming because they have not developed good work habits or study skills. It is no small wonder that students who were labelled as gifted in elementary school, often drop out of university because they are not doing well. This outcome is a tragic waste of potential that could have been developed through proper programming from the start.

Many gifted students are under served because their teachers do not know how to plan for them. Often enrichment activities are an afterthought, prepared and delivered only if the teacher has extra time. Because extra time is a rare commodity for teachers these days, many gifted students miss out on chances to explore topics in greater breadth and depth, develop research skills, and practise presentation skills. They may also fail to develop their leadership abilities and work/study ethics.

Simply put, like all students with special needs, gifted learners require accommodations, and their teachers are often at a loss as to how to plan for enrichment. The purpose of this guide is to provide you with approaches to gifted education, the means to identify gifts among your students, strategies for assessing your own attitudes and behaviors, and ways to plan units and activities for high ability students within your regular, elementary classroom.

Now is the time to make a concerted effort to focus on the needs of children with special abilities so that they can realize their potential, and experience joy in learning.

Cheryll Duquette

CHAPTER 1

Who Are High Ability Students?

The starting point in providing effectively for gifted children in your classroom is understanding more about giftedness.

Some students' abilities are easy to spot as being superior to those of their peers. Yet others are not as apparent. Perhaps some students in your class have characteristics similar to those presented here.

- Six-year-old Josh loves machines and gadgets; he wants to know how things work and has taken several tape recorders apart at home.
- Kirsty discovered debating when she was 11 years old and is the lead speaker on her team.
- Seven-year-old Tom hardly ever finishes work because he is always rubbing it out and starting over. His ideas don't seem to look as good to him on paper as they sounded in his head. His teacher says his work is fine, but he is not satisfied.
- Olivia, who is 5, does not get much written work done because she is always watching other people and taking in everything that is happening.
- Six-year-old Rachael pretends to like the picture books others are reading at school, but at home she reads long chapter books.
- Eleven-year-old Sophie would love a real friend who thinks like her but hasn't found one yet. However, she likes being alone because she can do the things she wants to do.
- Nine-year-old William challenged the teacher when another child was punished for not finishing an assignment. William believed that the work was inappropriate for the class.
- Sarah lies awake some nights worrying about war and the starving people she has seen on the TV news, though she is only 6 years old.
- Five-year-old Harry gets totally absorbed in drawing and will not stop when his mother or his teacher ask him to do so.

- Jenna, who is 4, knows the names of all the dinosaurs and can classify them by type and time periods.
- Seven-year-old Meredith makes jokes that only the teacher can understand.
- Nine-year-old Anna only needs to hear a tune once and she can hum it or pick it out on the piano.
- Ten-year-old Steve hates the fiction books studied at school but loves reading the encyclopedia and non-fiction books.
- Amanda, who is 7, suggested that the structure of the poetry they were writing was like the patterns they had been making in math, thus demonstrating a transfer of learning.
- Neil is only interested in Egyptology and wants to go to Egypt. He is 8.
- Marie taught herself to read by the time she was 4.
- Ten-year-old Linda is the chess champion at her school and can now beat her mother and father.
- Five-year-old Craig builds elaborate constructions out of blocks and won't let them be knocked down; he describes them in great detail to all who will listen.
- Jonathan is known and liked by almost everyone in the school. Not only is he friendly and empathetic, he is also a natural leader. He is 10 years of age.
- Michelle, who is 8 loves talking, problem-solving and art but has a specific learning disability in the areas of reading and writing.
- Seven-year-old Sanath recently came from Sri Lanka. Within six months he was fluent in English and making good progress in the second language taught at the school, even though it was his third.
- Twelve-year-old Emma is a deep thinker and knows her own strengths and weaknesses well; she evaluates her own work carefully and with great accuracy.
- Caroline, who is 10, is competing on a city-wide team in gymnastics.

All of these students have special abilities or gifts, but they are different from one another. It is easy to spot the 4-year-old who enters kindergarten knowing how to read. Other students require careful observation over time in order for us to identify their special gifts or talents. Defining special abilities, talents, or gifts is discussed in the next section of his planning guide.

CHAPTER 2

Defining and Approaching Giftedness

Before we discuss what constitutes giftedness, we need to look at some of the misconceptions about it. It is important to bring these out in the open and deal them. Here are some of the commonly held beliefs that lead to lost opportunities in our classrooms.

Myths About Giftedness

1. *Children can be gifted in only one area.* Some children perform at grade level in most subjects, but have a gift in one area, such as math, creative writing, or sports. These strengths need to be recognized and developed so that the student has the opportunity to reach his or her potential. However, there are also those students who perform beyond grade level in almost every subject. They are usually the ones with a total IQ score of at least 130 who need a range of curriculum modification to meet their needs. Therefore, some students may have a superior ability in one area, while others may be performing at a very high level in many subjects.

2. *It is élitist to provide differentiated programs for gifted students.* If we agree that everyone has an individual set of strengths and weaknesses and that students have a right to appropriate programs, then giving gifted students tasks that are designed to meet their needs is not élitist. It is providing them with what they need. Every student needs an appropriate program, whether it is at a higher or lower standard than grade level. Just because a student has a surplus of ability does not mean that we can afford to squander that ability through inactivity. Programming for him or her is not élitist; it is a matter of equity.

3. *Gifted children will make it on their own.* Unfortunately, gifted students who spend year after year occupying space in classrooms where they are unchallenged may fail to develop effective work/study habits, appropriate behaviors, and higher level thinking processes. Yes, in elementary and high school they will likely pass from year to year on a minimum of effort, but they will have been cheated out of an appropriate education. And when, sooner or later, they face an academic challenge, they may give up because they do not have the skills or attitudes that will lead them to success.

4. *All students are gifted.* We all have strengths. However, just because you have a strength, does not mean you are gifted. Students who are identified as gifted have undergone a battery of psychological tests as well as other screening methods to determine if they are gifted. Students labelled as gifted in many boards have a broad range of strengths that are about two years beyond grade level. A student with a high ability in one area, such as science would not likely be identified as gifted because he or she doesn't have a broad range of strengths that would produce the minimum total score required for the designation. Therefore, all students have strengths or gifts that need to be noticed and nurtured, but not all students are labelled as gifted.

5. *There are no gifted children in my classroom.* It is believed that up to 5 per cent of the population is gifted. It may be that in one academic year you have no students identified as gifted, but another year you may have two or three. However, you will always have students with specific abilities who require opportunities to do extension activities in order to explore those areas in greater breadth and depth.

6. *Students with a learning disability or physical impairment cannot be gifted too. Students from lower socioeconomic levels or different cultures aren't gifted.* Giftedness occurs evenly across all populations, including those with disabilities, those who have less money, and those who come from another culture. Unfortunately, sometimes teachers focus on the differences and don't see the gifts. A student with a learning disability may have a vast store of information about a variety of topics and have very effective oral skills. However, this same student may not be able to express his thoughts on paper. Unfortunately, sometimes we only see the weaknesses and not the strengths. Students who live in poverty or in other at-risk situations, may never have had the opportunity to extend their knowledge and skills, especially if their teachers have not looked beyond their clothes or the fact that they don't have school supplies. Sometimes these students are so focused on meeting their basic personal needs that the notion of their being

gifted never seems to occur to anyone. Finally, students coming from another culture are often overlooked as being gifted despite how quickly they pick up English (which may be their third or fourth language), and how advanced they are in math, simply because they are different. They don't fit the stereotypic idea of a gifted student: white, middle-class, and fluent in English.

When teachers observe their students carefully, they will find that all of them have strengths that need nurturing. They will also see that some students require enrichment because their gift or gifts are well beyond grade level. Moreover, they will realize that giftedness is found among all groups in the population.

Terms We Should Know

Before going on, we should define some terms associated with gifted education.

Gift(s)	strength or high ability in one or many subject areas, also includes intelligences, creativity, and talents
Gifted	the label given to a student who has a total score on an individually administered standardized IQ test that is in the superior range (usually 130 +), these students are usually performing at a high level in many subject areas
Talent	a highly developed ability in specific domains such as music, dance, visual arts, athletics, mechanical/inventiveness, information technology, and particular academic areas (such as language or math), talent is often observed in performance at a very young age
Creativity	a way of thinking that promotes original and unusual responses to everyday stimuli
Giftedness	a quality ascribed to a person who is identified through systematic assessment procedures as being gifted, having talent, or possessing creativity

There is no single definition of giftedness, as it varies from culture to culture and over time. However, in the western world over the last century, giftedness has traditionally been referred to as superior intelligence as measured by an individually administered standardized IQ test. Intelligence quotient (IQ) is calculated in the following way:

$$IQ = \frac{\text{Mental age}}{\text{Chronological age}} \times 100$$

People with a total score between 120 and 129 are considered mildly gifted. Those with scores between 130 and 139 are referred to as moderately gifted, and students with scores of 140 and beyond are labelled as highly gifted. In most boards of education, only those students with a total score of at least 130 on a standardized IQ test, such as the Weschler Intelligence Scale for Children (WISC - III) are labelled gifted. They are performing two or more standard deviations above the mean and are usually entitled to special programming, such as withdrawal programs for half or full days per week, or full-time segregated programs for gifted students. However, that doesn't mean that other students are lacking in abilities and talents. Unfortunately, under the present traditional approach, these students are often overlooked and miss out on opportunities to develop their strengths.

How Students are Identified as Gifted

1. Parents or teachers nominate them, and they are referred for assessment.
2. Assessment will likely include the following: an individually administered standardized IQ test, questionnaires for parents and teachers, and an examination of the student's portfolio of work and previous report cards.
3. The results of assessment are examined by a committee that includes the principal, teacher, special education teacher, the psychologist, the parents, and sometimes the child. The committee decides if the student meets the requirements to be labelled gifted (usually a total IQ score of at least 130), and decides upon placement for the student (regular classroom, partial withdrawal, or special segregated program).
4. An Individual Education Program (IEP) is developed for the student, and is reviewed once a year to ensure continued appropriateness.

Theories About Giftedness

In recent years, theorists have moved from viewing intelligence as a single score to seeing it as a number of different abilities. The work of Gardner (1983) is representative of this approach. His idea of multiple intelligences acknowledges that people have varying abilities and can demonstrate strengths in one or many of the areas. Gardner proposed a list of eight distinct and separate abilities or intelligences: linguistic, logical-mathematical, spatial, bodily-kinesthetic, musical, naturalist, interpersonal, and intrapersonal. Based on his idea, a student might have a particular strength in logical-mathematical intelligence, performing one year above grade level, but may have average ability in the other areas. This student will need enrichment in math, possibly through acceleration, to meet her needs. This type of enrichment would be provided by the classroom teacher, who would likely work with the special education teacher in the school to develop an appropriate program. Another student may have a high ability in music. To help develop this intelligence, the teacher might encourage him to write and perform a piece to demonstrate his grasp of the concepts in a particular unit.

> Spatial Intelligence may sometimes be linked to under-achievement, as this intelligence can be incompatible with the sequential learning emphasized in school. Spatial learners see the big picture without having to go through all the steps. They do well on tasks involving abstract concepts, visualizations, solving puzzles and problems, designing, constructing and mind mapping. However, they may do poorly at rote learning, phonics, spelling, and composition. Therefore, despite the potential weaknesses associated with spatial intelligence, it is necessary to recognize spatial intelligence as a strength and not a deficit.

Renzulli's model of giftedness from *What Makes Giftedness* (1979)

Renzulli (1977) proposed another view of giftedness, one that is based on characteristics rather than just areas of strength. He stated that no one single criterion should be used to identify students who are gifted, and proposed a model based on three interlocking clusters of traits: above-average ability (though not necessarily superior), task commitment, and creativity. According to this model, the interaction among the three clusters is needed for creative/productive accomplishment. Teachers may use this model as a basis for identification and program planning for gifted students. Further details will be provided in Chapters 3 and 4.

Creativity

Creativity is hard to define, since there is no agreement as to whether it is a category of ability or a way of applying intelligence which results in giftedness. However, some definitions explain creativity as new and original ways of doing or thinking of things. Creativity involves divergent thinking which includes the following:

- fluency of ideas or producing a number of responses to a given stimulus,
- flexibility or shifts in thinking from one category to another,
- originality or unusual and clever responses, and
- elaboration or the addition of details to basic ideas or thoughts.

Creative students may be able to generate many solutions to a problem, including some that are unusual, yet possible. They may also be able to concentrate for long periods of time on special projects, often preferring to work alone. Creative students may ask a lot of questions and have a well developed sense of humor. They often do well on tests with an apparent lack of effort. Although there is no definite link between creativity and academic giftedness, it appears that a person identified as creative usually has a minimum IQ of 120. Unlike academic giftedness, creativity is hard to quantify. As a result, many teachers find it difficult to identify these students, particularly if they do not demonstrate a high level of ability in creative writing or visual arts. Regardless, teachers can plan classroom activities that stimulate creativity, some of which will be discussed later.

Emotional Intelligence

Goleman (1996) proposed that emotional intelligence contributed significantly to successful relationships. Included in emotional intelligence are the following: self-awareness of feelings, strengths, and weaknesses; being able to manage moods; being motivated towards goals; having empathy; and being able to persuade or lead others. As you can see, there is an overlap between emotional intelligence and Gardner's interpersonal and intrapersonal intelligences. Having gifts in emotional intelligence may also involve having a strong sense of justice, acute sensitivity to moral and ethical issues, and intensity of feeling. This can sometimes result in defying adult authority, if an injustice is perceived (Piechowski, 1997).

Talent

Unlike creativity, talent is easily observable as it is shown in above average performance, and frequently at a young age. Hence, it is usually identified by parents and coaches/teachers in the particular area. Talent areas include: music, dance, visual arts, athletics, mechanical/ inventiveness, and particular academic domains (such as language or math). Bloom (1985) found that there were three characteristics associated with the development of talent no matter what the area:

- willingness to devote great amounts of work (practice, time, effort) needed to achieve,
- ambition to reach a high level of attainment in the field, and
- ability to learn rapidly new techniques, ideas, or processes in the area of talent.

Bloom also noted that talent was nurtured at an early age by parents who went out of their way to obtain special instruction and to provide encouragement. The enthusiasm of the parents seems to be critical in developing talent to a very high level. The role of the classroom teacher is to celebrate the talents of specific students and to put into place ways for those talents to be developed further.

Nature or Nurture?

Are intelligence, creativity, and talent inherited or are they developed in a particular environment? Over time, studies of twins who had been adopted and the strong similarities between them and their birth parents point to the importance of heredity. However, researchers also make a strong case for the significance of environments that help to identify, support, and develop abilities. Barbara Clark (1997) sees giftedness as an interaction of both heredity and environment:

> The development of giftedness is the result of an interactive process that involves challenges from the environment that stimulate and bring forth innate talents, capabilities, and processes . . . We either progress or regress intellectually; stability or maintenance of a fixed quantity of intelligence is not possible. Giftedness, as a label for a high level of intelligence, is a dynamic quality that can be furthered only by participation in learning experiences that challenge and extend from the point of the child's talent, ability, and interest.

A Responsive Environment

Identifying precocious students is easy. They perform at a high level at school, are articulate, outgoing, and motivated. But what if an able student is not motivated at school, is underachieving and a behavior problem, has a learning style inconsistent with the general style of the classroom, speaks a first language which is different from that of the teaching language of the classroom, or has a disability? We may not detect this student's gifts so easily. In some cases, such students may be viewed as nuisances or obstacles to the progress of the entire class. Olivia, Rachael, William, Michelle, and Sanath may be underachieving, hiding their abilities, being labelled as behavior problems, or may have the kinds of abilities that are not so easily recognized/valued.

Identification and programming are linked and are both continuous processes.

Responsive Environment (school, classroom, and home)

allows

Special Abilities to Become Apparent

which helps to

Identify Needs

which leads to

Appropriate Programming Options

which are part of the

Responsive Environment

The key to identifying giftedness among children lies in providing an environment which is responsive to their needs. A responsive environment is one which is supportive of diversity and individual differences and where relationships are cooperative and respectful. It is also emotionally safe, cognitively stimulating, and characterized by trust and acceptance. In this sort of responsive and caring environment, students' abilities are likely to flourish and be noticed.

The implications of a responsive environment are as follows:

- It shows all students that they are valued. Their intelligences, talents, and creativity are welcomed, and therefore they can be themselves. Diversity is expected and accepted. In this environment they won't have to hide their gifts for fear of ridicule or resort to bad behavior out of restlessness or sheer boredom.
- Teaching methods and ways for students to demonstrate that they have mastered the material are varied. Teachers then have opportunities to observe students' performance in their preferred intelligence.
- The input of parents and caregivers is encouraged, so that the school receives as much information as possible, and from the people who know their children best.

Will This Mean More Work for You?

Once a student's gift or gifts have been identified, you have a moral responsibility to develop an appropriate program to develop the student's full potential.

Not likely. Most elementary teachers already have a positive attitude towards diversity, incorporate a variety of teaching and assessment methods, and try to involve the parents as much as possible. Is recognizing the intelligences and developing an individual program required for every student in the class? Yes and no. Yes, you should make careful observations of each student to determine their strengths. No, you do not have to develop a completely individualized program for each one. Usually, a student will have strengths in one or two areas, which can be easily accommodated through extensions to the lesson. These extensions are commonly found in the teacher guides that accompany the texts you already use. Many teachers regularly incorporate these ideas into their lessons and units. However, for those students who are working well beyond grade level in one or more areas, you will have to adapt the classroom curriculum to meet their needs. Doing this is not as difficult or time-consuming as it may seem at first. Moreover, the consequences of ignoring your students' strengths are far more time-consuming and counter-productive than an appropriate response to them in the first place. In Chapter 4 you will learn the steps of adapting units and lessons for gifted learners. But first, you will need tools for identification and some general programming ideas.

CHAPTER 3

Identifying Students' Gifts and Gifted Students

Some students will demonstrate their abilities during the first day of school. These will be the people who provide detailed answers to all your questions, ask their own questions, and complete the individual seatwork carefully and quickly. However, there will be other students whose academic strengths, intelligences, or talents won't become apparent for a while. Regardless, it is important that you begin observing your students early in the school year so that you can better understand them as individuals and provide effectively for their needs.

Data Sources

The hallmark of a good teacher is knowing the strengths and weaknesses of each student, helping with the weaknesses, and nurturing the strengths.

Information about your students will come from three main sources: your own observations, their parents, and the students themselves. All three sources are important in order to develop a complete picture of a student's abilities. Teachers can use the instruments presented in this chapter, as well as anecdotal records, class test results, and work samples. Parents may also provide anecdotal information. If you arrive at the point that you feel a referral for psychological testing is required, then parents must give their consent and will likely be asked to complete rating scales. The students may be involved by completing inventories, self-nominations, and through discussions about their accomplishments outside of school. The table on page 20 summarizes the sources and types of data.

WHO	HOW
TEACHERS	• create a responsive environment • observe using checklists or rating scales of characteristics • observe and record anecdotally • note results of classroom tests • evaluate products / examples of work / performances — group and individual • take note of competition results
PARENTS/ COMMUNITY	• being involved in school/ home conferences • responding to questionnaires • filling in rating scales of characteristics • providing anecdotal information • showing examples of children's products
STUDENTS	• filling in interest/ strength inventories • self-nominating for programs • achieving awards outside of school

Judy: A Case Study

Judy's teacher made some careful observations of her performance over a period of two to three months. Although the exact frequency Judy had demonstrated the specific behaviors was not noted, the teacher had observed them several times.

Identification Tools

On the next pages are tools you can use to identify the abilities of your students. The process of knowing a student's strengths and weaknesses begins early. Start in September to collect data on each student, record test results, note the extent to which a student meets expectations, collect work samples, and write short anecdotal reports. Also, refer to the following lists of characteristics to determine each student's strengths. Pay particular attention to those who are achieving at a very high level and who have not been referred for assessment or identified as being gifted. Then record these observations on an *Individual Profile Form* for each student. A black line master is found in the Appendix. It is important that you review the lists with each of your students in mind,

JUDY: A CASE STUDY

The abilities of 9-year-old Judy have been identified in a variety of ways by her teacher. It has been noted that she shows:

- **many of the indicators of general ability**

  identified by her class teacher using a checklist of characteristics of general ability.

- **a high level of interpersonal and intrapersonal intelligences**

  identified by teacher observation and parent information. For example, Judy cares deeply about issues; is reflective, has empathy.

- **high abilities in oral language, reading, written language and research/work skills**

  identified by superior language scores from the standardized achievement test; publication of stories, editorials and articles in the school newspaper; self-nomination for the debating club.

- **many characteristics of creativity**

  identified by teacher and parent observation of such things as: originality in written work, challenge of the status quo in regard to environmental issues; enjoyment of periods of solitude.

- **a high level of task commitment**

  identified by teacher observation and parent report of Judy's self motivation in investigating real issues, writing, debating.

including the ones who are behavior problems, require remediation, or have cultural/socioeconomic differences so as not to focus on the weaknesses and overlook the strengths.

This process occurs over time, and you should observe a characteristic more than once to report that a student demonstrates it. For further information, ask the parents about their children: what they enjoy about school, their activities outside of school, and if appropriate, the competitions they have entered. This could be done during the parent/teacher interviews after the first report card is issued. As well, you could also schedule a short interview with each student early in the year and talk to them about their favorite subjects and activities.

Indicators of Above Average Abilities

A. General Ability Indicators
- Displays logical and analytical thinking
- Is quick to see patterns and relationships
- Is able to understand complex concepts and abstract ideas
- Achieves quick mastery of information
- Easily grasps underlying principles
- Likes intellectual challenges
- Jumps stages in learning
- Is able to see areas for further study (find problems)
- Is able to solve problems
- Reasons things out for self
- Formulates and supports ideas with evidence
- Can recall a wide range of knowledge
- Independently seeks to discover the why and how of things
- Is concerned about moral and ethical issues; strong sense of justice
- Has a high level of sensitivity and empathy

B. General Ability — Multiple Intelligences
- Bodily-kinesthetic   physical movement and knowledge of use of the body
- Interpersonal   relationships and communication; understanding others
- Intrapersonal   knowledge of own thinking and emotions
- Linguistic   use of words and language
- Musical   sensitive to rhythm, tonal patterns, performance/composition
- Naturalistic   curiosity about natural world; ability to classify flora and fauna
- Spatial   comprehends the visual world; creation of mental images

C. Specific Abilities
- Oral language
- Reading
- Written language
- Languages other than English
- Mathematics
- Science
- Technology
- Construction/mechanical
- Information technology
- Athletics

- Health
- Visual art or crafts
- Dance
- Drama
- Music
- Social studies
- Research/investigation
- Leadership
- Culturally valued abilities
- Other

D. Underachievers

The following are possible traits of students with gifts who are underachieving. Demonstrating some of the following traits does not mean that the student is gifted. It means that you should continue to observe the student with the view that the behaviors currently exhibited may mask certain gifts. Keep an open mind.

- Being disruptive, off-task (day dreaming, fidgeting), manipulative
- Showing feelings of inferiority, low self-confidence, or expectations of failure
- Having a subtle sense of humor
- Having a strong sense of justice
- Showing a strong sense of determination
- Having interests outside of school
- Having difficulty with written expression
- Asking a lot of questions
- Completing work infrequently
- Being an English-as-a-second-language learner

E. Creativity Indicators

- Fluency of ideas but also able to select what is important
- Flexibility and originality of thought
- Willingness to challenge the existing way of doing things
- Openness to that which is new and different
- Intensely curious, speculative
- Adventurous, willing to take risks
- Sensitive to detail, aesthetic qualities
- Unusual interests
- Ability to tolerate solitude
- Keen sense of humor
- Complexity of personality

The Lists of Indicators of Above Average Ability have been compiled from a wide variety of sources including McAlpine and Reid (1996), Gardner (1983), Ramos-Ford and Gardner (1997), Goleman (1996), and Renzulli and Reis (1985).

F. Task Commitment Indicators
- High level of interest, enthusiasm, fascination, and involvement in problem or chosen area of study
- Intrinsic motivation to complete a project/assignment
- Perseverance, endurance, determination, hard work, dedicated practice
- Self-confidence in ability to achieve
- Setting high standards for one's work

Below is a case study of Sam. His teacher used the lists of above average ability and made the observations which are presented after the case study. A black line master of the form used by Sam's teacher is found in the Appendix.

Sam: A Case Study

Sam is 7 years 2 months of age, in Grade 2. In school he is particularly interested in, and also good at, math, problem-solving, drawing, constructing, and expressing himself orally. He sometimes makes jokes that only the teacher understands. When the class or a small group is engaged in problem-solving, Sam is able to contribute a lot of ideas to the discussion. He cannot always explain his math reasoning, but appears to make mental leaps and finds unusual ways to solve problems. However, he often computes the answer incorrectly because he wants to be first to finish. His printing is messy, he can read reasonably well (though not by choice), and he does not like to write creative stories.

Sam gets on well with other children and with adults. Out of school he also loves to discuss and argue issues with adults. Sam spends hours making elaborate constructions mainly out of Lego and loves to know how things work. He plays chess and board games with anyone who will play, sometimes beating his parents.

INDIVIDUAL PROFILE FOR   Sam

GENERAL CHARACTERISTICS	MULTIPLE INTELLIGENCES	SPECIFIC ABILITIES	STRONG INTERESTS	INDICATORS OF CREATIVITY	EVIDENCE OF TASK COMMITMENT
quick to see patterns	linguistic (oral)	chess	chess	fluency of ideas	chooses to construct, draw, play chess at home and school and concentrates for a long time on them
understands complex concepts	logical/mathematical	oral language	board games	flexibility	
quick mastery of information	spatial	maths problem-solving	building Lego models	challenges existing way of doing things	
grasps underlying principles		drawing	drawing	openness to new and different ideas	
likes intellectual challenge			talking	curious	
jumps stages in learning				adventurous, risk taking	
problem-finds and problem-solves				sensitive to detail, aesthetics	
reasons things out for self				keen sense of humor	
seeks to discover how and why of things					

© 2003 *Your Top Students* by Shirley Taylor. Pembroke Publishers Limited. All rights reserved. Permission to reproduce for classroom use.

INDIVIDUAL PROFILE FOR _Sam_

MEANS OF IDENTIFICATION: _Teacher observation – general characteristics (from school-wide identification sheet), specific abilities. Self-nomination for chess club. Parent information – interests, abilities, task commitment._

LEARNING NEEDS: _Opportunities to respond to tasks in own style i.e. oral, visual–spatial, hands-on; not just sequential or written. Opportunities for engagement with other children with like abilities – oral, artistic, chess, problem-solving. Opportunities to extend skills in areas of ability._

SUGGESTED PROVISIONS

WHAT	WHEN/WHERE
Oral discussion, problem solving, debate	Classroom language groups
	Cross-age Year 3–5 Oral enrichment group Term 2
Drawing skills & techniques	Cross-age Workshop with parent/artist: half day for 6 weeks
	Using techniques from workshop in classroom
Choice of style of product for work	Classroom tasks/projects/independent studies
Play chess & board games	Friday afternoon electives with others who choose to do so
	Monday lunchtime club

RECORD OF PROVISIONS

© 2003 _Your Top Students_ by Susan Taylor. Pembroke Publishers Limited. All rights reserved. Permission to reproduce for classroom use.

Looking Back and Moving Forward

In this chapter we have discussed the process of identifying students' abilities, which involves collecting data from a variety of sources and recording the appropriate indicators on the Individual Profile Form (as seen in Sam's case study). In Chapter 4 we will examine various programming options for high ability students and re-visit the cases of Judy and Sam.

Learning, Planning, and Providing

This chapter will help you learn how to interpret the observations you have recorded and to plan programs for students needing extensions and enrichment.

Interpreting Your Observations

Once you have your data in front of you, it may become obvious that a particular student is performing two or more years above grade level in one or more subjects and is doing above-average work in the others. You may also have observed many of the characteristics shown in the lists presented in Chapter 3. From your data, you may conclude that this student could be gifted. If this is the case, read her file to determine if IQ testing has occurred and if this student has an IEP. It may be that she arrived from another board and programs are not yet in place for her. If there is evidence of previous testing that shows the student has superior abilities (total IQ score of 130 or above) and has an IEP, then you should speak to the principal immediately about providing her with appropriate accommodations. If the student's file shows that no previous IQ testing has been done, discuss your observations with either the principal or special education teacher. If it is decided that the student should be assessed, the parents and student (depending on her age) should be invited to meet with you to discuss your board's assessment procedure and possible placement options. The placement options could be the regular classroom with enrichment, the regular classroom with enrichment and partial withdrawal, or a full-time segregated classroom. The result of this meeting may be that the family does want to go ahead with the testing (which could be done by the board or by a psychologist

Remember that you are not alone in preparing extension and enrichment activities for your high-ability students: talk to the school's special education teacher and your board's consultant about enrichment ideas.

in private practice). The family could also decide that they do not like the placement options and decline the opportunity for assessment. In this case the student would remain in the regular classroom, and the teacher would provide enrichment.

On the other hand, from your data you may notice that a student has some above average abilities; however, strengths in the academic areas do not appear to be more than two years beyond present grade level. This is the case with both Judy and Sam, whose learning needs would likely be accommodated by the classroom teacher. We will discuss how to meet the needs of both students shortly.

General Placement and Program Planning Options

When deciding on placement and program options, schools, parents, and students need to know the range of options that will meet the needs of high ability students. These have been organized into three categories as found below: grouping, pacing, and other. Grouping by performance or aptitude can be done at a board, school, or classroom level to help high ability students meet their needs. Flexible pacing can be used to move a student more quickly through specific subject area or an entire grade. Finally, other program accommodations can be made that involve the community, such as mentorships, competitions, and special programs.

Options for High Ability Students

Grouping

Segregated classrooms	Students from across the board are congregated in a classroom for all of their instruction, which is focused on the needs of high ability students.
Resource room or withdrawal programs	Special programs are provided for students who are pulled out of their regular classroom once or twice a week for enrichment activities. The classroom teacher must also provide enrichment during the times when the student is in his or her class.
Cross-age/grade grouping	The school, or grades in a school, are divided for language and/or math into groupings by ability. Therefore a younger student could be placed with a group of students in a higher grade for reading.
Within class grouping	An heterogeneous class is divided into three groups according to ability (low, middle, high), usually for language and math.

Cluster grouping	Four to six high achieving students in a classroom are grouped together to do assignments or projects.

Pacing

Early entrance	The student enters elementary, middle, or high school earlier than his peers.
Grade acceleration	The student either skips a grade (e.g., goes from Gr. 2 to Gr. 4 without doing Gr. 3), or does two grades in one year (e.g., Grades 3 and 4 in one year).
Self-paced instruction	The student is accelerated in a subject area. This is usually done in math because it is organized sequentially.
Compacting course material	The content of a course is compressed to give more time to the student to pursue individual projects. The teacher must decide what parts of the curriculum will be eliminated (usually through administering a pre-test), and substitute more appropriate content.

Other

Mentorships	The student is paired with a mentor from the community who shares her interest in a particular area (e.g., artistic and scientific fields)
Competitions	The student is encouraged to enter competitions, such as science fairs or story/poetry writing contests.
Special Programs	Some communities have special classes on a wide variety of topics given by local experts. There may also be "mini enrichment" courses given by universities for gifted learners. Summer programs that are brief but have intense learning experiences may also be available.

Approaches to Enrichment

Renzulli's Enrichment Triad

Renzulli (1977) proposed a model of giftedness, which was described in Chapter 2. It may also be used to guide the development of enrichment experiences for high ability students (Renzulli & Reis, 1985). The primary goal is to develop the student's ability to research, investigate, and solve real problems. This model is composed of three distinct steps or types of activities.

Type I activities are designed to awaken the students' interest in the topic. They could include videos, field trips, lectures from community experts, and other introductory learning experiences that will help students identify further areas of study.

Type II activities consist of training in research and problem-solving methods. Brainstorming, scientific method, self-awareness, and values clarification are types of processes that may be taught to students in a systematic way.

Type III activities include individual or small group investigations in which students research topics selected from the Type I activities. The emphasis is on developing a product, solving a real-life problem, or producing an original performance for live audiences.

Self-directed Learning

Donald Treffinger (1975) developed a curriculum model that addresses students' individual abilities to manage independent projects. He proposed using contracts that are written at three levels of self-direction:

Level 1   A student will select a topic for research from a small number of options given by the teacher. Specific time lines and expectations for performance (rubrics) are provided. The teacher plays a larger role in evaluating the product than the student.

Level 2   The teacher and student brainstorm topics for investigation and mutually decide on one, as well as the time lines and criteria for success (rubrics). The teacher and student share the role of evaluating the work.

Level 3   The student decides on the project, time lines, and rubrics. The teacher approves of the plan and plays a minimal role in evaluating the work, the larger proportion being assumed by the student.

A sample of a contract that could be used for a Level 3 self-directed project is found in the Appendix.

Problem-Based Learning (PBL)

Problem-Based Learning provides students with opportunities to practise learning about real-life problems while working in small groups. The problems serve to spark the students' interest and as a basis for learning about a unit of study. The students are presented with an ill-formed real-life problem, and are made stakeholders in the situation. For example, the students are told they are planners who must develop a strategy for their city to reduce its garbage accumulation. The teacher then coaches them on the thinking processes needed to solve the problem (Stepien, Gallagher, & Workman, 1993). Students must think critically and analytically, as well as find and use appropriate learning resources, as they discover the real problem and develop the solution.

This method of enrichment may be used as a unit on its own or after the students have demonstrated they have met the expectations of the regular unit through curriculum compacting.

Tiered Lessons

A tiered lesson accommodates the needs of different groups within a class by providing differentiated assignments. Usually, a teacher will have three groups: high, middle, and low. For example, when studying a novel the activities for a low reading group may be to answer questions on plot, character, setting, and theme. The middle group would do the same work, plus a dramatization of a particular event. The high group would demonstrate that they know the basics of the story and be given opportunities to compose an alternate ending, write a poem about the story, develop a board game based on the novel, or write an editorial related to an issue raised in the story.

Some teachers also prepare tiered activities at science learning centres in order to differentiate the content of the unit for all learners in their class. They write clear instructions for each group, which are color coded. The lower group may do a basic task, such as developing an electrical circuit for a light bulb. A middle group could do the same activity, as well as connect a number of small lights in parallel wiring. A higher group could extend their learning by working with electro-magnets. They could also investigate different types of power plants or be given the problem of finding an efficient source of power for a city or factory.

Bloom's Taxonomy

Bloom's (1956) taxonomy of educational (cognitive) objectives provides a basis for distinguishing between higher and lower order thinking. Bloom's classification of educational experiences includes six categories: knowledge, comprehension, application, analysis, synthesis, and evaluation. Knowledge and comprehension are considered to promote lower order thinking because they include activities based on recall of information. The remaining four are considered higher order thinking because students are required to think more deeply about the information. Most curriculum is written at the knowledge and comprehension level, and Bloom's taxonomy has been used for years as a means of differentiating and enriching it for high ability learners. However, that doesn't mean that gifted learners do not have to know and comprehend the basic information.

Bloom's taxonomy was designed for planning objectives and evaluation, but it is also a useful framework for planning units. For example, in a primary unit on communities found in the social studies curriculum, the teacher may present basic ideas and terms to the

Bloom's Taxonomy

Level	Definition	Task	Product
Knowledge	remembering, recognition, recall of ideas	define, identify, list, label, match, name, outline, recall, reproduce, select, state	define vocabulary, state dates and factual information, tests and quizzes, workbook exercises
Comprehension	show an understanding of the main idea or basic concepts in the curriculum	explain, predict, give example, infer, interpret, paraphrase, rewrite, summarize, translate	translation (words or numbers), summaries, predicting consequences and effects
Application	apply what is known in new and real situations	change, compute, demonstrate, manipulate, modify, operate, predict, prepare, produce, show, solve, use	applies theory to practical situation, problem solving, constructs charts and graphs, demonstrates correct usage of a method or procedure
Analysis	ability to break down material to understand its parts and how it is organized	categorize, diagram, distinguish, infer unstated assumptions, recognize point of view and bias, relate cause and effect, subdivide	assignments in which students must know the parts and show relationships between parts in words or diagrams, distinguishes between fact and fiction, states causes and effects
Synthesis	ability to combine elements and parts from many sources into a new and original whole	combine, compile, compose, create, design, generate, modify, organize, reorganize, revise, write	research paper with many sources, a plan proposal for research, debate, an editorial, a model for classifying objects or ideas, an original creative story (or poem or music), integrates learning from different areas to solve a problem
Evaluation	ability to make judgements about the value of ideas, works, solutions, methods, and materials	appraise, compare, conclude, criticize, discriminate, judge in terms of criteria, justify, support	judges and supports opinion on the following: the logical consistency of written material, the adequacy of conclusions, the value of a work (art, music, writing) using specific criteria, self-assessment

From Benjamin S. Bloom et al *Taxonomy of Educational Objectives* © 1984. Published by Allyn and Bacon, Boston, MA.
Copyright © by Pearson Education. Reprinted by permission of the publisher.

students (knowledge and comprehension). At the application level, students could be asked to draw a map of their own community. At the analysis level, students may compare and contrast two or more communities. At the synthesis level, they can create a play about important people in their community. At the evaluation level, students can share their opinions about their own community's services and how to improve upon them (Eby & Smutny, 1990). Over the years, teachers have used this taxonomy for planning objectives/expectations, evaluation, learning experiences, and questioning for individual lessons.

Planning for the Regular Classroom

Now that you have read an array of possible program options, it is hard to know how to begin and how to develop curriculum that meets the needs of the students with gifts or who are gifted.

Where Do You Start?

As described earlier, a teacher needs to create a responsive environment that takes into account students' needs. A responsive environment permits a student's abilities and talents to be demonstrated, and ensures that accommodations are in place to meet individual needs. Where do you start? With yourself. On page 36 is a questionnaire and planning sheet for you to fill in. Remember that nobody is perfect. If you answer "yes" to some of the questions, you're doing much to provide a responsive environment for children with special abilities already, but you might also see areas for improvement.

Learning and Teaching Strategies

Now that you are aware of your own strengths and have thought about ways you can improve programming for high ability students, let's consider the four building blocks of curriculum differentiation. These are content, process, product, and assessment.

Content refers to what the students should know, understand, and be able to do at the end of the unit. You can provide enrichment for everyone in your class by having personal enrichment sheets on hand for quick research on a topic, extension activities that are found in teacher guidebooks, computer software related to the topic, or a list of web sites that students can visit. (See the Appendix for the Personal

DO I PROVIDE A RESPONSIVE ENVIRONMENT?	YES	TO SOME DEGREE	NO	ACTIONS TO TAKE
Are high ability students in my class happy? Do they want to come to school?				
Do I keep an open mind when a parent says their child has a special ability or needs more challenge?				
Do I provide for a wide range of abilities in students from all cultural groups?				
Do I focus more on strengths than weaknesses even if children are underachieving or have specific learning difficulties?				
Do I acknowledge that it is OK for a high ability student to know more than I do about some things?				
Do I allow for a variety of learning styles and multiple intelligences?				
Do I ensure that students are challenged to work towards their full potential rather than cruising along?				
Do I make sure that high ability students don't repeat and practise what they already know?				
Do I provide opportunities for high ability students to learn at their own pace?				
Do I allow for in-depth study of areas of interest?				
Do I allow personal goal-setting and encourage self evaluation?				
Do I encourage creativity, risk-taking and original responses?				
Do I encourage higher level thinking?				
Do I allow for flexibility of grouping including the choice of working alone?				
Am I aware of the social and emotional needs of high ability students and do I make appropriate accommodations?				

PERSONAL PRIORITY FOR ACTION: . . . .

© 2003 *Your Top Students* by Shirley Taylor. Pembroke Publishers Limited. All rights reserved. Permission to reproduce for classroom use.

Enrichment Exploration black line master.) For students in need of further challenge, you can plan individual and small group projects incorporating Treffinger's self-directed learning, Renzulli's Type II and III learning, Bloom's higher order thinking, or problem-based learning. These projects should be ones that are more abstract and complex than those for the other learners. They should include real-life problems, or new products that the students have made for specific audiences, and integrate a variety of subject areas.

Process refers to the speed in which students learn the content. High ability students should have opportunities for acceleration and compacting. Math is usually the subject area in which students are accelerated because content is presented sequentially. Compacting the curriculum by giving the high ability students a pretest, teaching what absolutely must be learned, and assigning a reduced number of questions (every second one or just the hard ones) are ways to compact the curriculum. With the time that is left over, the students with high abilities can work on their individual projects.

Product is what students produce to demonstrate what they have learned. For students with high abilities, this may include a choice of presentation, transformation of information, and communication to an audience. When examining what these students will produce to demonstrate their learning, consider Gardner's multiple intelligences and Bloom's taxonomy.

Assessment refers to how you will determine to what extent the students have met the expectations for the unit. When preparing your rubrics, bear in mind the level four requirements, making them appropriate for the high ability learners. You will also need to explain your expectations to these students before you begin teaching the unit. Ensure that the rubric descriptors include demonstrations of deeper thought, more thorough research, independence, originality, and products geared towards a particular audience. Also include opportunities for the high ability student to do some self-assessment on the process of doing the project, the resources on hand, and the outcome of the project. As well, schedule time each week to conference with the student to discuss the project and share the enthusiasm.

The Building Blocks of Curriculum Differentiation			
Content	Process	Product	Assessment
Enrichment for Everyone – personal enrichment sheets – extension activities – computer software and the Internet – Renzulli: Type I and II – Treffinger: Level 1 and 2 – Bloom: knowledge, comprehension, application – tiered lessons **Students with Superior Abilities** – individual and small group projects – Renzulli: Type III – Treffinger: Level 3 – Bloom: analysis, synthesis, evaluation – tiered lessons	– acceleration – curriculum compacting – groupings – PBL	– Bloom: analysis, synthesis, evaluation – Gardner: multiple intelligences	– rubrics – self-assessment – student/teacher conferences

Including High Ability Students

Now that we have the building blocks of differentiation and know about enrichment, we can look at the steps in planning a unit to include high ability students. As we have noted, one of the reasons high ability students don't seem to be sufficiently challenged is that their needs are often considered *after* the unit has been prepared. You can do a better job of accommodating the needs of all learners at the very beginning, when you are in the initial stages of planning. In this chapter, you will learn a four-stage method of unit planning that includes provisions for high ability learners. The steps in this model are initiating, reviewing/gathering, planning, and assessing. Each is described below.

Four steps in developing a unit: initiating, reviewing/gathering, planning, and assessing.

1. Initiating

- Read the curriculum documents and know the expectations for the unit.
- List the concepts, information, and skills students are to know for the unit (in layman's language).
- Identify your own knowledge gaps, list areas you must research.
- Decide on the culminating activity.
- List how each expectation will be assessed. (Consider Gardner's multiple intelligences, tests, projects, portfolios, and self-assessment.)
- List lesson topics for the unit keeping in mind the expectations and the skills required for the culminating activity.
- Beside each topic list teaching methods (e.g., small group, individual research project, experiment, learning centres, problem-based learning, teacher demonstration, lecture, etc.).
- List other subject areas that might be integrated.
- List resources you have for each lesson topic (e.g., print material at varying reading levels, videos, web sites, CD-ROMs, manipulatives, etc.).

Enrichment

- Beside each lesson topic or groups of topics list extension and enrichment activities. (Consider Bloom's taxonomy, Gardner's multiple intelligences, Treffinger's self-directed learning, Renzulli's Type II and III activities, and problem-based learning.)
- Discuss the unit and lesson topics with the high ability students. Plan individual and small group projects and decide on appropriate resources, assessment roles, and methods.

2. Reviewing and Gathering Resources

- Review materials and resources on hand to assess suitability to lesson topics.
- Write the materials to be used for each lesson topic.
- Note lessons in which there are no resources, inappropriate resources, or insufficient resources.
- Gather new materials to fill these gaps. Ask colleagues, consult a board resource centre, check the Internet, go to the school library, visit public and university libraries, and ask local resource people.
- Add the new resources and materials to each topic.

Enrichment

- Discuss and share resources and materials that are appropriate for the individual/small group projects already chosen by the students.
- Encourage students to find other resources for their projects.

3. Planning Lessons

- Plan a lesson(s) for each topic. Include how you will compact the curriculum, list extension activities that are appropriate for all learners, plan questions to include higher order thinking, open-ended questions (no specific answer), and divergent questions (more than one solution to a problem).

Enrichment

- Prepare a place in the classroom (e.g., a table at the back of the room) on which to display and store extension activities.
- Prepare a work area for high ability students to do enrichment projects, if required.

4. Assessing the Effectiveness of the Unit

- Plan how you will assess whether students felt they learned a lot, worked hard, worked effectively in groups, and enjoyed the activities.

Enrichment

- Plan to include the points above, as well as whether the students extended their knowledge and skills beyond the regular curriculum, had sufficient and appropriate resources, had enough time to work on their projects, and had opportunities to initiate and direct their learning.

As you can see, this model of unit planning involves spending a lot of time at the beginning to sort out what has to be taught, how it will be evaluated, lesson topics, and possible resources. All of these components need to be nailed down before the lesson plans can actually be written. And, there is provision for planning for enrichment in each stage of the model so that inclusion occurs at the outset. Feeling overwhelmed? Don't be. Your hard work at the outset will save effort in the long run. And In the Appendix there are Unit Planning and Lesson Topics Planning templates that will help you organize your planning activities.

CHAPTER 5

Ideas for Your Classroom

Incorporating Independence

The students in your classroom (even the high ability ones) will be working at different levels of independence. Treffinger's self-directed learning model can help you develop differentiated activities to accom- modate different levels of independence. There are four levels of self-direction in this model, which makes it possible for all of the class to be working on a topic with varying degrees of depth and independence (Treffinger, 1975 in Maker & Neilson, 1995).

1. *Teacher-directed*   At this level, those who need firm guidance will carry out activities set by the teacher. It may be that all students will do some of these activities at the beginning of a unit then the more independent ones will move to other steps.

2. *Some choice within teacher-created options*   The teacher still sets the activities, but the students choose what they will do and in which order. The content may be the same for all or it can be differentiated so that there are higher level activities for some students.

One way of doing this is to use **hopscotch contracts** (p. 42). If the content is designed for different groups, each student must do each step but in their own time. If the content is the same for all, high ability students could miss out the first two steps (compacting) and do the rest of the steps. The steps could be based on Bloom's taxonomy.

If they can cope easily with this they can use a **tic-tac-toe grid** (p. 43) which allows a choice of three out of nine activities as well as the order in which they do them.

These simple contracts may be used in any subject area as well as across the curriculum. They can be based on content or could focus on practising skills such as taking notes, interviewing and approaches to work including different styles of gathering information or styles of presenting work. They may also incorporate the multiple intelligences by including activities using the full range of intelligences.

The following hopscotch could be used by junior or middle primary high ability students, individually or with a partner. They need sound reading and thinking ability and a degree of independence.

They could:

- do each step
- do number 1 and three others
- do number 1, one from 2, 3, 4 and two from 5, 6, 7, 8

The hopscotch activities incorporate the use of communication skills, information skills, work and study skills. They are based on the different types of thinking in Bloom's taxonomy.

This hopscotch could also be used by all students with an interest in dinosaurs, if reading material at a suitable level is provided and if manageable steps are chosen.

Hopscotch Contract: Dinosaurs

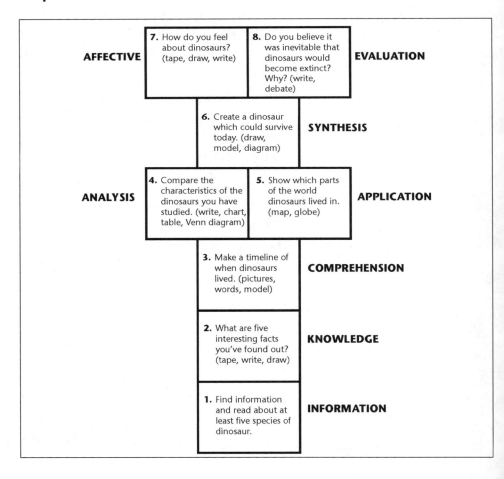

3. Teacher and student create options together   Once students have the skills to manage choice and their own time, allow for more open-ended activities and more input to the learning activities from them. Continue to teach further independent learning skills, such as devising a good open-ended question. Create activities together or specify non-negotiables and allow them to devise the rest of the activities. Students can create tic-tac-toe menus based on their interests or have some free choice squares in a teacher-made grid. Negotiate timeframes and encourage some self and peer evaluation.

The following tic-tac-toe grid would be suitable for middle or upper primary students and can provide an opportunity for those with special abilities interested in leadership to explore issues in depth and also become involved in leadership. Students could choose to work individually, with a partner, or in a group of three.

Tic-tac-toe Contract with Leadership as the Key Concept

Make a study of the reasons why people become leaders. Give examples of individuals who have become leaders in each of these ways.	What style of leader would you like to be? Why?	Write several generalizations (i.e. statements that you believe always apply) about leadership.
Plan a leadership initiative in which you could be involved in your school. Try to "sell" the idea to your teacher.	**FREE CHOICE**	Choose a great leader to study. Set yourself an open-ended question to find out about that person.
Design a concept map with leadership as the central concept.	What are the qualities of a good leader? Rank them in order of importance and justify your ranking.	Define and explore an issue of gender / culture / race and leadership.

Choose a line of three to do.

4. Student-directed   Students set their own questions, carry out the independent learning, self-evaluate and present the results but still always negotiating this with the teacher.

A **goalpost contract** can be used. (This technique could initially be learned as a group). The steps are:

- On a large piece of card, write your question.
- Draw goalpost of favorite sport.
- Cut out balls for that sport and number them.
- Write each step in order on separate balls.
- Blu Tak balls on chart.
- Put each ball through/over goal as step is achieved.

A diary can be helpful for student-teacher communication so the teacher can see what help is requested on reading the diary after school.

An example of an investigation that a high ability student at the primary level could carry out is as follows:

QUESTION: Were toys the same in the past as they are today?

STEPS:
1. Make up questions to ask students in order to find out what toys they play with.
2. Make up questions to ask adults to find out what toys they used to play with.
3. Ask questions of 10 teachers, parents or grandparents — record on tape.
4. Ask questions of 10 students — record on tape.
5. Draw a graph to show toys today / past.
6. Tell the other students about similarities/differences and show the graph.

Treffinger's model of self-direction can be used in conjunction with the Enrichment Triad Model outlined on pages 31-32. Type II Renzulli skill learning fits with steps 2 and 3 of Treffinger's model. Treffinger's student self-directed learning step can be incorporated with Renzulli's ideas for Type III investigative work.

Allowing for increasing degrees of self-direction differentiates the process of learning and the content can be higher level or self-selected. A range of products can also result.

Original products or performances can represent a synthesis of information the student finds into a new form. (Note that "original" means original for that student at that time, not necessarily new to the world! However, he or she may go on in adulthood to be a real creator i.e. a transformer of knowledge in a domain.)

Products may include:	
• letter	• oral presentation
• newsletter item	• map
• song	• model
• music	• crafts
• "how to" book	• timeline
• role play	• computer-generated table
• story for publication	• painting
• dance	• graph
• advertisement	• demonstration
Audiences for these products/performances may include:	
• teacher	• community group
• students in class	• older students
• elderly peole	• readers of school newsletter
• a student buddy	• an e-mail pal
• mentor	• parents

Discovery Learning

Do students in your class sometimes say they are bored? Well, encourage them to **THINK**. Don't tell — let them discover. For example try teaching an alternative to regular multiplication. This could be to a group of students who have mastered long multiplication easily; they need a new challenge. The "telling" way would be to show them an example on the board and tell them how ancient Egyptian multiplication works. The "discovery" way works like this: Write up two examples on the board:

~~25 x 26~~	20 x 13	
50 x 13	~~40 x 6~~	
~~100 x 6~~	80 x 3	
200 x 3	160 x 1	
400 x 1		
650	260	

Ask them to figure out how the system works. They will need to try more examples of their own to see if their theory works. (Can **you** see how the system works? See explanation below!)

They can then investigate related questions such as why remainders are not used, why some examples take more steps than others, what happens when bigger numbers are used. Students end up doing lots of computation without being asked to!

---

* Explanation of ancient Egyptian multiplication:
Numbers in left column are doubled.
Numbers in right column are halved and remainders left out.
Whenever the numbers in the right column are even, the row is crossed out.
To find the answer, the numbers not crossed out in the left column are added together.

Conceptual Learning

Concept maps, in which students diagrammatically represent relationships between concepts, can be used at the culmination of a unit of work to draw understandings together, or sometimes at the beginning to determine prior knowledge.

The key concept of the topic is written in the middle of a large piece of paper and related concepts are identified by either the teacher or the students. A good way to do this is to write each concept on a small piece of paper. They are then arranged on the large page with arrows drawn between them and joining words and phrases written in. Much discussion ensues as to where the concepts should go and how they relate. That is why having them on small pieces of paper is helpful so that they can be physically moved around.

Concept Map with Beauty as the Central Concept

Concepts being studied by the class could be extended to draw out generalizations or themes, which could then be investigated. Some possible themes are *heroes* in various cultures and in different eras; *discovery* as a catalyst for change; and *cooperation* often requires compromise, which can be positive or negative.

Specific investigations may appeal to able students from the perspective of ethics, cultural studies, or an interest in global issues. Examples of topics that may be explored from a variety of lenses include new technology, prejudice, conservation, extinction, cultural diversity, and animal rights. How global issues may be manifested locally might also be explored, which could lead to questions such as — what can we do as individuals? This approach could help to change a student's feeling of powerlessness to one of believing he or she can do something to make a difference.

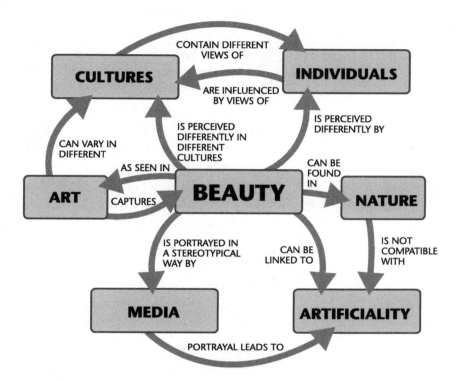

Returning to Judy and Sam

Let's return to the two case studies of Judy and Sam and examine some possible accommodations.

Judy showed many of the indicators of general ability, as well as a high level of linguistic, interpersonal, and intrapersonal intelligence. She had specific abilities in oral language, reading, written language, and research/investigation. Judy also demonstrated many of the characteristics of creativity and a high level of task commitment. Given this information, we can interpret her learning needs to be as follows:

- to compact the time spent on the basics
- to have the opportunity to study topics in depth
- to have the opportunity to select her own topics of study
- to have the opportunity to work on real issues with others who feel strongly about them
- to have the opportunity to interact orally with others
- to have the opportunity to use self-assessment of her work.

Most of Judy's needs can be accommodated in the regular classroom through compacting, self-directed learning, Type II and III learning activities, and problem-based learning. Issues and problems that relate to the school or community might be a focus for some of her projects. To provide for the need to interact orally, Judy should be encouraged to continue participating in the debating club and perhaps a mentor could be found to develop her writing.

And Sam?

Return to page 25 to review Sam's individual profile. You can see that he too shows many of the indicators of general ability and has linguistic (oral), logical/mathematical, and spatial intelligences. Sam demonstrates specific abilities in oral language, math (problem-solving), and drawing. His interests include chess and other board games, building with Lego, drawing, and discussing. Sam also shows many indicators of creativity and task commitment.

Like Judy, most of Sam's needs can also be accommodated in the regular classroom.

Sam needs to be able to respond to tasks in his own style, which is oral, visual-spatial, and hands-on, and not just sequentially or in written form. He also needs to interact with other students with like abilities and interests (discussing, art, chess, constructing, and problem-solving). As well, Sam needs to extend his skills in the above areas.

Sam's teacher can do the following to provide for his learning needs:

1. Use multiple intelligences to give all students the opportunity to learn and respond to some tasks in a variety of ways, such as drawing a diagram, writing the answer, or making a model. Tic-tac-toe grids could also incorporate choice of multiple intelligences activities. Providing choice in assignments and the presentation of them will help Sam (and others) demonstrate his understanding to the best of his abilities. As well, Sam should be allowed to arrive at the answer in his own way in subjects such as math, where he may not follow the usual steps.
2. For some tasks Sam should be grouped with students of similar abilities and interests so that he can interact orally and solve problems. He should also be encouraged to join the school's chess club.
3. Given Sam's many abilities, he would benefit from the following: a curriculum unit based on a theme that integrates three or four subject areas; being able to discover patterns and investigate in math rather than being told and then made to practise; a chance to do hands-on activities and not always written work; and an art project that could be a self-selected area of study.

Assessing Your Accommodations for High Ability Students

When using an existing unit or developing a new one, you can ask the following questions to ensure that you have provided those who need enrichment with activities to challenge and motivate them. If at least some of the elements can be incorporated, that is an excellent start.

1. *Are there enrichment activities for all students?*

When developing your units, plan to include quick extension-type activities that could be used by all students. These can be found in your teacher guide books or you may choose to provide independent research forms for students to do some superficial investigation of a topic, problem, or issue. High ability students will require more extensive planning in which they may be involved to determine the topics, types, and assessment methods of self-directed projects.

Ideas for an Enrichment Table for Your Classroom

All students should have opportunities to engage in enrichment activities. These can be extensions to your curriculum or ones that challenge even your brightest students. The following are ideas for your enrichment table:

- Extension activities for your content areas — For science you could have directions to simple experiments and the materials needed to perform them, in math you could put out manipulatives (to count to 100), pattern blocks, and tangrams. You could also prepare a folder with web sites related to the science and social studies units the students are studying.
- More advanced reading materials — Print material (fiction and non-fiction) could be related to a unit being studied or an issue being discussed in class. These materials could come from the school library, public library, or your own collection.
- General resources — These would include a set of encyclopedia and copies of *National Geographic*, *Scientific American*, or any other subject-related magazine. These materials may be obtained at garage sales.
- Vocabulary building — You can cut out the Word Power pages from old *Readers' Digest* magazines and place them in a folder along with crossword puzzles, and any other games you can find.
- MENSA worksheets — These contain interesting problems that are bound to keep your high ability students interested for a long while.
- Personal Enrichment Sheets — Personal research can be done by all students in an area of interest that is related to a topic being discussed in class. They are quick to complete and usually involve only one source of data. Students can submit them for extra credit. (See the Appendix for the Personal Enrichment Exploration black line master.)

---

2. Are there opportunities for students to demonstrate their knowledge in a variety of ways and using different intelligences?

Not every unit will lend itself to permitting students to demonstrate their learning in a full range of styles and intelligences. However, ensure that there is a sufficient variety of learning activities and assignments for all students. While doing individual research projects is an excellent activity for high ability learners, a steady diet grows tiring. Consider varying projects and presentation formats. For example, use oral and written types, or combine them using a multi media approach, create a poster, or write and produce a dramatization. Students could also create a web site, an I-movie, or board game. These projects could be done individually or in small groups.

3. Does the unit allow for depth of thinking, such as the exploration of concepts, themes, issues, and cross-curricular ideas?

High ability students need opportunities to explore ideas in greater depth and breadth, and they need to go beyond recalling information and acquiring basic skills. Ensure that high ability students (and others) have opportunities to engage in activities that require higher order thinking skills.

4. Are there opportunities for students to choose their assignments?

Providing choices of methods of presentation (e.g., oral or written), difficulty of assignment (as in tiered lessons), and type of product (such as research paper, poem, sculpture, or dramatization) can be a way to differentiate the curriculum for all learners.

5. Are there parts that can be compacted to allow for exploration by the high ability students?

These students do not need to re-learn material they already know and practise skills they have mastered. At the beginning of the unit, give them a pre-test in order to determine their gaps in knowledge and skills. You may be surprised at how much they already know. Then teach the unknown sections of the curriculum to the high ability students. The faster pace you create through compacting will result in more time for these students to do individual or small group investigations and projects.

6. Are creative products possible?

Ensure that within the unit there are opportunities for students to produce variations of an assignment, and to give original answers which may or may not have to be supported with evidence. Including activities from Bloom's higher levels of thinking and divergent thinking permits opportunities for unique and varied responses.

7. Does the unit allow for varying levels of initiative?

Students work at different levels of independence. Some have ideas and are self-starters who simply need the resources. Others will require more structure and monitoring, particularly if they are underachieving or have just begun doing enrichment activities.

8. Is self-assessment incorporated?

All students should reflect on how they worked and the outcome of their activities. They should then be required to list how they can make improvements for another time.

9. Is there anything in the unit that is motivating to gifted underachievers?

Consider the interests of these students and, if appropriate, try to incorporate something in those areas. You might also permit students to have choice over assignments, thereby giving them some sense of control. For self-directed assignments, some underachieving gifted students may require a Level 1 approach with much structure, support, and encouragement to achieve success.

10. Is there the possibility of mobility, if necessary?

Decide if all the resources will be contained in the classroom or if students will have to go to the library or computer room. If there will be some movement, you may have to make special arrangements to use the school facilities. You may also be able to take the class on a field trip to a museum, or go outdoors to collect specimens, or take them on a nature walk. Some assignments may also require work outside of school, such as interviewing a grandparent, as part of a unit in social studies.

11. Is there consideration given to the social and emotional needs of high ability students?

Ensure you know which of your high ability students need to develop leadership abilities, social skills, and self-confidence. Occasionally, you can incorporate small group activities in which you have selected the groups based on ability or interest. Sometimes, a student will learn how to take a leading role in working with others to complete a project and may find a friend in the process.

Social/Emotional Development

Here are more ideas on how to create a classroom that addresses the social and emotional needs of high ability students.

No one can make you feel inferior without your consent

Eleanor Roosevelt

This is great advice but usually not realized until adulthood. Surprising to many, is the fact that gifted students often do feel inferior because inferiority equates to difference or being rejected, of not being part of the popular or "in" group. As well, with their heightened sense of social justice and greater awareness of other people's needs, gifted students often experience confusion and a sense of being alone.

What can the teacher do to enhance social / emotional development? The answer is: *RESPONSIVE ENVIRONMENT RESPONSIVE ENVIRONMENT RESPONSIVE ENVIRONMENT!!!*

A Positive Teacher Attitude

The most important thing is your attitude. Show you like this student. Try not to use words like *over* sensitive, taking things *too* seriously or being *too* idealistic. Emotional giftedness is not *too* much; it is emotional depth and intensity. Gifted students not only think differently from their age peers; they can also feel differently.

- **Recognize that students may be extroverts or introverts** — One is not better than the other; it is a different personality style. Extroverts learn and think by talking with others, they like to share ideas, answer quickly, do not hide their feelings, are spontaneous, and like to have many friends. Introverts process ideas internally and may not want to share them, are very private people, need time alone, are very reflective, probably have a few special friends, and may feel lonely in large groups of people.
- **Help the loner find a friend** — Try pre-arranging the groups for work with partners or small groups so that the gifted student has a person with whom to work who shares abilities or interests. You could also arrange the desks in your class in rows of two desks together or in groups of four. This could help the gifted student find a friend or friends. Having a friend is important because students who are constant loners are targets for bullying.
- **Remember high ability students don't have to act "gifted" all the time** — they are people. It is hurtful to use their ability against them such as "If you're so smart, why can't you tie your shoelaces?" or, "You might be in the enrichment class but you can't be that smart if you don't know this". A student can talk eloquently during the day about various theories of why dinosaurs became extinct but might still need to sleep with "blankie" at night. As you can see, gifted students develop asynchronously: academically they may be years ahead of

their peers, but physically and emotionally their development may be age appropriate.

- **Don't allow peers to use "put down" language** — We don't allow racial slurs or name-calling for those with disabilities, and we can't permit gifted students to be labelled as "nerds" or worse. As well, try to monitor your behaviors towards these students so that peers don't refer to them as "teacher's pets."

- **Create a classroom atmosphere** that encourages all students to take academic risks. Encourage all students to try new things and make mistakes without fear of ridicule. You might also model appropriate behavior when a mistake happens.

- **Recognize qualities** such as humility, patience and sensitivity as being important and nurture them. A way of developing and using these qualities is in the service of others such as in peer mediation, producing books for younger students, and conducting concerts in retirement homes.

- **For some students, leadership increases their self-esteem** and also allows an outlet for service to others. It may be leadership of younger students, teaching new skills to the class such as in art, or leading a special cultural group. However, not all high ability students want to be leaders. There are also different forms of leadership, some of which are quiet and behind the scenes, rather than up front. Learning about leadership is also worthwhile with such content as conflict resolution, problem-solving, planning and studying the qualities of leaders.

- **Remember that the class rules apply to gifted students** — Sometimes people excuse rude, inconsiderate, and rule-breaking behavior on the basis that the student is gifted. Avoid doing this. Gifted or not, the classroom rules should be applied and common courtesies should be required. Create a classroom where everyone is respectful to one another.

- **As these students may be intellectually capable** of understanding adult humanitarian issues and feel the weight of the world on their shoulders, they need outlets to do something or they may feel powerless. Thus, real community projects and studying real issues need to be part of their curriculum.

- **Conceptual learning also contributes** to emotional development through the discussion of such concepts as prejudice, sensitivity, persistence, power. It helps students to develop awareness of their own values and the values of others.

- **Like-ability grouping is necessary some of the time.** High ability students need to interact with others of similar ability so that they do not always feel different, can form friendships and experience intellectual stimulation. These groups may be mixed age at times. It may allow them opportunities to find true peers. Peers are not always

Leadership is not sending the gifted student who has completed the work to give 1:1 assistance to another student who is struggling with seat work. This is acting as an unpaid paraprofessional. Leadership involves taking a leading role in the completion of a group activity, sharing results or a project with the class, or solving a class problem (e.g., how to construct the sets for the class play).

. . . real community projects and studying real issues need to be part of their curriculum.

the same age; it is more to do with a person to whom you are drawn, with whom you have something in common, who understands you and accepts you.

- **Adult mentors who accept gifted students** and are interested in them can also help them to view their difference as positive rather than negative. A mentor who shares a strong interest with a student can help him or her to see that it takes time to develop skills to a professional level, thus relieving the pressure to perform perfectly without practice. Mentors can help students to strive for excellence, not perfection. A mentor of one's own ethnic group and gender can be powerful.

- **Recognize that when a student challenges** you, it may be a strong sense of justice coming to the fore. Don't be upset by it or see it as defiance; give your reasons for what you did or said. Even be prepared to admit ocassionally that you were wrong! Sometimes humor (not sarcasm) can defuse a situation also.

- **Listening to them may be particularly important** for some high ability students if other classmates do not share their interests. You may need to set aside a few minutes a day to listen and discuss ideas on an "adult" level.

- **Be prepared to learn from them or with them**. Some students will know more than you do about certain things. Remember they don't know all that you know and they won't have as much wisdom as you do about the world but they might have a passion area that they know an enormous amount about. Let them share that passion with you.

- **Acknowledge and value their strengths**. For instance, if a student is good at developing original ideas, is orally articulate, and has talent in art, but also has difficulty with reading and writing, ensure that both *strengths* and weaknesses are noted. Sometimes, teachers just focus on the deficits and ignore the strengths. However, the student will gain self-esteem from opportunities to shine in areas in which she excels.

- **Allow for creative outlets** such as personal diaries, painting, poetry, drama and music.

- **Practise reflective listening** so that you reflect back to the student their concerns without stating any judgement. This often lets the student open up more and elaborate because you are showing that you are listening. Acknowledging their feelings does not necessarily mean agreement.

- **Allow the student to engage in role play** in a small group situation. This may include communication skills, assertiveness training and social skills.

- **Facilitate personal growth plans**. The student thinks about:
  — Something I would like to change or develop.
  — A goal based on this.

You may need to set aside a few minutes a day to listen and discuss ideas on an "adult" level.

— What are the roadblocks to get around?
— Who are the people who will help?
— What are the steps I'll take?
— How am I managing on each step?

- **Practise creative problem-solving.** Teach your high ability students a way of solving social problems that may arise. For example, they may complain that they have no friends or that everyone insults them by calling them nerds. A model you could introduce for solving social problems (and other types) could be as simple as the following: 1) define the problem, 2) brainstorm possible solutions, 3) think of the outcomes of each possible solution, 4) select the best solution, 5) implement your solution, and 6) evaluate about your choice and think about what you have learned. You might spend some time teaching this model with the entire class or individual students.

- **Allowing students to learn cognitively** in a variety of ways, choosing their own preferred way when learning new material, or carrying out an investigation of a topic or issue in depth, contributes to emotional development through acceptance of individuality. For example, if certain students learn well visually and spatially, let them see what needs to be done. Give them the big picture. Let them visualize the end product or let them watch someone else perform the task. Allow movement and hands-on learning for a kinesthetic learner. Create chances for a verbal student to talk, for a musical student to create or listen to music, for a naturalist to engage with natural topics and classify, for someone who thinks logically and scientifically/ mathematically, to reason and experiment. Remember some people like to (even need to) learn with others, work in a group, discuss ideas. Others prefer to work alone and reflect on what they are doing.

Most of these suggestions can be carried out in the classroom. Some are planned strategies; others are just ways of interacting with very able students. Some could be facilitated in a wider school context when appropriate, such as mixed age group role play, leadership activities, and working on real issues.

Relating to Parents

What parents most dread is the "brick wall syndrome." They just want to be listened to and have their knowledge about their children recognized. If a parent arrives and says her/his child is very able but seems to be a little bored or unhappy at school, you could:

— be defensive
— fight back
— see it as a slur on you
OR
— listen
— keep an open mind

- Understand what the parents may have experienced such as meeting brick walls earlier, being labelled as pushy, seeing their child unhappy through teacher attitude or peer ridicule, having their child's abilities seen as an inconvenience in the school, being kept on their toes constantly by a child who, from an early age has always been on the go, thirsting for knowledge.
- Agree to observe closely and get back together.
- Provide specific observation and classroom assessment data. Ask the parents to provide specific information such as examples of what their child says, makes, writes or paints, questions they ask, interests, how they choose to spend their recreational time.
- Develop some shared goals.
- Report on positives; don't just wait for negatives.

Parents want what is best for their children. The offer of a partnership will be music to their ears and working co-operatively with families ultimately benefits the student.

Conclusion

As you have seen, accommodating the needs of students with gifts and those who are gifted can be done in the regular classroom. You have read about different approaches to enrichment, the identification of abilities, the development of unit plans, and specific techniques that can be incorporated into your classroom practice. However, a positive attitude on the part of the teacher goes a long way in contributing to the development of a responsive environment in which students' strengths come to the fore and learning needs are met. With an open mind, a sense of empathy, and a differentiated program you *can* make a difference in the lives of *all* of your students.

Appendix

INDIVIDUAL PROFILE FORM FOR _____

GENERAL CHARACTERISTICS (HIGHLIGHT CHARACTERISTICS WHICH APPLY)	MULTIPLE INTELLIGENCES (HIGHLIGHT IDENTIFIED INTELLIGENCES)	SPECIFIC ABILITIES	STRONG INTERESTS	INDICATORS OF CREATIVITY	EVIDENCE OF TASK COMMITMENT
• logical & analytical thinking	• Bodily-kinesthetic				
• quick to see patterns & relationships	• Interpersonal				
• understands complex concepts & abstraction	• Intrapersonal				
• quick mastery of information	• Linguistic				
• grasps underlying principles	• Logical – Mathematical				
• likes intellectual challenge	• Musical				
• jumps stages in learning	• Naturalist				
• problem-finds and problem-solves	• Spatial				
• reasons things out for self					
• formulates & supports ideas with evidence					
• can recall a wide range of knowledge					
• independently seeks to discover how and why of things					
• concern for justice, moral & ethical issues					
• sensitivity & empathy					

© 2003 *Your Top Students* by Shirley Taylor. Pembroke Publishers Limited. All rights reserved. Permission to reproduce for classroom use.

INDIVIDUAL PROFILE FOR _____

MEANS OF IDENTIFICATION:

LEARNING NEEDS:

SUGGESTED PROVISIONS
WHAT   **WHEN/WHERE**

RECORD OF PROVISIONS:

© 2003 *Your Top Students* by Shirley Taylor. Pembroke Publishers Limited. All rights reserved. Permission to reproduce for classroom use.

Learning Contract for Independent Study

Title of Project: _____

Description of Project (Include the purpose and the process for gathering data.):

_____

_____

_____

_____

_____

_____

_____

Type of Product (Describe what will be produced.):

_____

_____

Criteria for Evaluation:

_____

_____

Breakdown of Marks:

_____

_____

Due Date: _____

_____   _____
Signature of Student and Date   Signature of Teacher and Date

Reproduced from *Students at Risk* with permission from Cheryll Duquette.

© 2003 *Your Top Students* by Shirley Taylor. Pembroke Publishers Limited. All rights reserved. Permission to reproduce for classroom use.

Unit Planning

Name of Unit:_____   Grade: _____

Initiating

Expectations, concepts and skills:

Expectation	Concepts/Information required to meet the expectation	Skills required to meet the expectation

Areas I need to research:

Culminating activity:

Student assessment methods:

Related disciplines:

Reviewing/Gathering
List sources of materials and information

Planning Lessons for Gifted Students (See also the Lesson Topics Planning Sheet.)

- Extensions
- Opportunities to compact material
- Questioning and activities with higher order thinking skills, open-ended

- Individual/group projects
- Place for extension materials in classroom
- Place for enrichment projects in the classroom

Assessing the Unit
Methods of unit assessment for all students

Methods of assessing the effectiveness of the unit for students requiring enrichment

2003 *Your Top Students* by Shirley Taylor. Pembroke Publishers Limited. All rights reserved. Permission to reproduce for classroom use.

Lesson Topics Planning Sheet

Unit: _____   Grade: _____

Lesson Topics	Expectations	Assessment	Teaching Methods	Resources	Extension/Enrichment Activities

© 2003 *Your Top Students* by Shirley Taylor. Pembroke Publishers Limited. All rights reserved. Permission to reproduce for classroom use.

Personal Enrichment Exploration

Focus Topic or Question:

_____

_____

What Was Learned:

_____

_____

_____

_____

_____

_____

_____

_____

Other Topics or Questions That Arose:

_____

_____

Resources Consulted (Books, Internet, People, etc.):

_____

_____

_____

_____

Reproduced from *Students at Risk* with permission from Cheryll Duquette.

© 2003 *Your Top Students* by Shirley Taylor. Pembroke Publishers Limited. All rights reserved. Permission to reproduce for classroom use.

Recommended Reading for Children

Below is a list of just a few books which may appeal to able children on an emotional level.

Picture Books For Young Children

A Bit of Company by Margaret Wild (1991)
Amazing Grace by Mary Hoffman (1991)
Anno's Counting Book by Mitsumasa Anno (1977)
The Cat in the Hat by Dr. Seuss (1957)
Chrysanthemum by Kevin Henkes (1991)
Communication by Aliki (1993)
Dragon Quest by Allan Baillie (1997)
Ebb's New Friend by Jane Simmons (1998)
Feelings by Aliki (1984)
Good Night Moon by Margaret Wise Brown (1947)
Henry and Amy by Stephen Michael King (1998)
The Mole Sisters and the Piece of Moss by Roslyn Schwartz (1999)
More, More, More, said the Baby by Vera B. Williams (1990)
The Most Wonderful Egg in the World by Heine Helme (1983)
The Paperbag Prince by Colin Thompson (1992)
The Paperbag Princess by Robert Munsch (1980)
The Snow Lambs by Debi Gliori (1995)
The Snowy Day by Ezra Jack Keats (1962)
The Very Best of Friends by Margaret Wild (1989)
The Very Hungry Caterpillar by Eric Carle (1969)
The Very Last First Time by Jan Andrews (1985)
The Whale's Song by Dyan Sheldon (1990)
Where the Wild Things Are by Maurice Sendak (1963)
Wilfred Gordon McDonald Partridge by Mem Fox (1984)
Yo! Yes? by Chris Raschka (1993)

Novels For Young Readers

Biddy Alone by Wanda Cowley (1988)

The Butterfly Lion by Michael Morpurgo (1996)
Catwings by Ursula Le Guin (1990)
The Chalk Box Kid by C Bulla (1987)
Charlotte's Web by E B White (1963)
The Chicken Gave it to Me by Anne Fine (1992)
From the Mixed-up Files of Mrs Basil E Frankweiler by E L Konigsburg (1967)
Homesick, My own Story by Jean Fritz (1987)
Hugo and Josephine by Maria Gripe (1962)
Mouse Time by Rumer Godden (1995)
Much Ado About Aldo by Johanna Hurwitz (1978)
My Father's Dragon by Ruth Stiles Gannett (1948)
Shadrach by Meindert de Jong (1957)
The Secret Life of Owen Skye by Alan Cumyn (2002)
The Shrinking of Treehorn by Florence Parry Heide (1975)

Picture Books For Older Children (8-9 Years Upwards)

Arabella by Wendy Orr (1998)
Ernest and Ethel by Raymond Briggs (1998)
The Hockey Sweater by Roch Carrier (1979)
How to Live Forever by Colin Thompson (1995)
Looking for Atlantis by Colin Thompson (1996)
The Lost Thing by Shaun Tan (2000)
Rose Blanche by Christophe Gallaz (1996)
The Silver Pony by Lynd Ward (1973)
The Staircase Cat by Colin Thompson (1998)
Stormy Night by Michele Lemieux (1999)
Tower to the Sun by Colin Thompson (1997)
Voices in the Park by Anthony Browne (1999)
Way Home by Libby Hathorn (1994)
Weslandia by Paul Fleischman (1999)

Books For Older Readers (10 +):

The Boy in the Burning House by Tim Wynne-Jones (2000)
Bridge to Terabithia by Katherine Paterson (1978)
A Cage of Butterflies by Brian Caswell (1992)
Come Sing, Jimmy Jo (1985)
Dreamslip by Brian Caswell (1994)
Dust by Arthur Slade (2001)
Fat Four Eyed and Useless by David Hill (1987)
The Freak by Carol Matas (1997)
The Golden Compass by Philip Pullman (1995)
The Hollow Tree by Janet Lunn (1997)
Holes by Louis Sachar (1998)
Just Juice by Karen Hesse (1998)

Little by Little by Jean Little (1987)
The Lottie Project by Jacqueline Wilson (1997)
The Music of Dolphins by Karen Hesse (1996)
Out of the Dust by Karen Hesse (1997)
The Outside Child by Nina Bawden (1989)
The Root Cellar by Janet Lunn (1981)
A Single Shard by Linda Sue Park (2001)
Stars Come Out Within by Jean Little (1990)
Stone Fox by John Reynolds Gardiner (1980)
A Time to Fly Free by Stephanie Tolan (1983)
Underrunners by Margaret Mahy (1992)
A Wrinkle in Time by Madeleine L'Engle (1962)

Older children often like to read biographies and autobiographies. These can be of people past or present from a variety of cultures. Reading about these people who have made recognized contributions to society can contribute to self-understanding.

Books Written Especially For Gifted Children

Adderholdt-Elliot, Mariam (1987) *Perfectionism: What's bad about being too good?* MN: Free Spirit

Delisle, James and Galbraith, Judy (1987) *The gifted kids survival guide II (for ages 11-18)*. MN: Free Spirit

Galbraith, Judy (1987) *The Gifted Child's Survival Guide (for ages 10 and under)*. MN: Free Spirit

Galbraith, Judy (1992) *The gifted child's survival guide (for ages 11-18)*. Victoria: Hawker Brownlow

Hipp, Earl (1985) *Fighting invisible tigers. A stress management guide for teens*. MN: Free Spirit

References

Bloom, B. (1985). *Developing talent in young people*. New York: Ballantine Books.

Clark, B. (1997) *Growing up gifted*. 5th edition. New York: Merrill

Davis, G. & Rimm, S. (1994) *Education of the gifted and talented*. 3rd edition. Needham Heights, MA: Allyn & Bacon

Eby, J. W. & Smutny, J. F. (1990). *A thoughtful overview of gifted education*. Toronto: Copp Clark Pittman.

Gardner, H. (1983) *Frames of Mind*. New York: Basic Books.

Goleman, D. (1996) *Emotional intelligence: Why it can matter more than IQ*. London: Bloomsbury

Maker, J. & Neilsen, A (1995) *Teaching models in education of the gifted*. 2nd edition. Austin, TX: Pro-Ed

Ramos-Ford, V. & Gardner, H. (1997) *Giftedness from a multiple intelligences perspective.* In N. Colangelo & G. Davis (Eds) Handbook of gifted education. 2nd edition. MA: Allyn & Bacon

Renzulli, J. (1977). *The enrichment triad model: A guide for developing defensible programs for the gifted and talented.* Mansfield Center, CN: Creative Learning Press.

Renzulli, J. & Reis, S. (1985) *The schoolwide enrichment model: A comprehensive plan for educational excellence.* Mansfield Centre, CT: Creative Learning Press

Silverman, L. K. (1988). Gifted and talented. In E. L. Meyen & T. M. Socratic (Eds.), *Exceptional children and youth: An introduction* (3rd ed. pp. 263-291). Denver: Love.

Stepien, W., Gallagher, J., & Workman. (1993). *Problem-based learning for traditional and interdisciplinary classrooms.* Journal for the Education of the Gifted, 16(4), 338-357.

Treffinger, D. (1975). *Teaching for self-directed learning: A priority for the gifted and talented.* Gifted Child Quarterly, 19(1), 46-59.

Web Sites

Organizations

Council for Exceptional Children (www.cec.sped.org)
GT World (www.gtworld.org)
National Association for Gifted Children (NAGC) (www.nagc.org)
National Foundation for Gifted and Creative Children (www.nfgcc.org)
National Network of Families with Gifted Children (NNFGC) (www.come.to/gifted)
TAG Family Network (www.tagfam.org/)
World Council for Gifted and Talented Children (www.worldgifted.org)

Teacher Resources

www.hoagies.gifted.org
www.eagle.ca/~matink/teacher.html
www.argotlibrary.com/gandt.html
www.eskimo.com/~user/kids.html
www.odysseyofthemind.com

Articles On-Line

www.cfge.wm.edu/Publications/Articles
www.ericfacility.net/ericdigests
www.library.umass.edu/subject/education/speced

Listings and Descriptions of Journals on Gifted Education

www.ericed.org/fact/gt-journals
www.hoagiesgifted.org/journals

Index